Splash

words by Jill McDougall
illustrated by Bill Wood

"Get on the log," said Wolf.

"This looks like fun," said Bear.

The log went fast.

Splash, went the mud.

"Yuck! Look at my nose," said Bear.

6

"It's just mud," said Wolf.

The log was stuck.

"Push," said Wolf.

"Yuck! Look at my feet," said Bear.

"It's just mud," said Wolf.

Bear pushed hard.

"Not so fast," said Wolf.

Splash, went Wolf.

"Yuck! Look at me," said Wolf.

15

"It's just mud," said Bear.